I0816205

TABLE OF CONTENTS

Sight Words.......... 2

Words to Know.......... 3

Index.......... 16

A Pelican Book

Teaching Tips for Caregivers and Teachers:

Research shows that one of the best ways for students to learn a new topic is to read about it.

Before Reading

- Read the title and predict what the book will be about.
- Read the "Words to Know" and discuss the meaning of each word.
- Read the back cover to see what the book is about.

During Reading

- When a student gets to a word that is unknown, ask them to look at the rest of the sentence to find clues to help with the meaning of the unknown word.
- Motivate students with praise and encouragement.

After Reading

- Discuss the main idea of the book.
- Ask students to give one detail that they learned in the book.

Sight Words

all	get	on
around	go	some
by	have	water
carry	I	

Words to Know

cars

decks

engines

ferryboat

seats

I get around by **ferryboat**.

ferryboat

All ferryboats have **engines**.

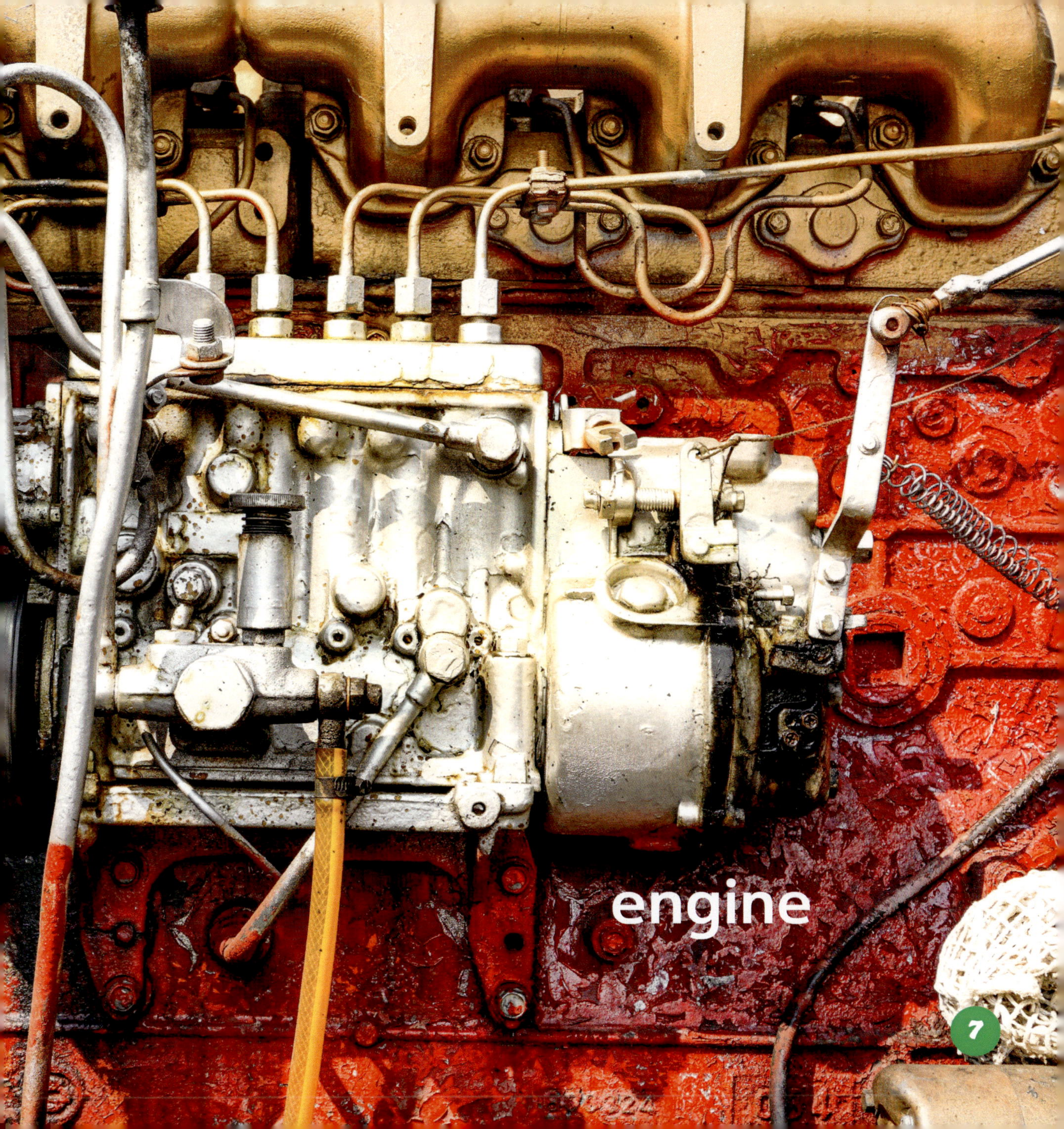

engine

All ferryboats have **decks**.

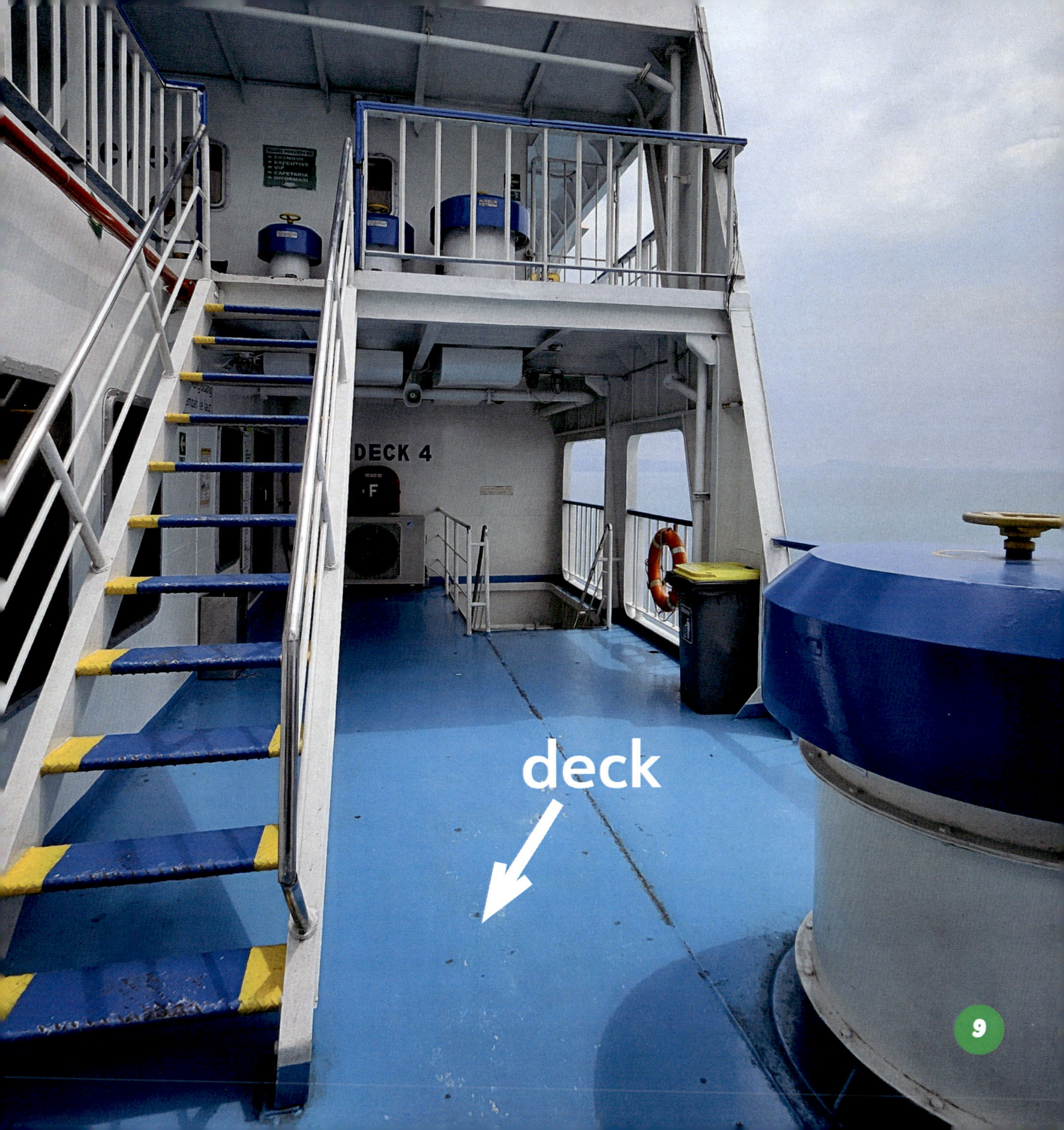
DECK 4
deck

seats

Some ferryboats have **seats**.

Some ferryboats carry **cars**.

car

All ferryboats go on water.

Index

cars 12, 13
decks 8, 9
engines 6, 7
seats 10, 11
water 14

Written by: Ryan Earley
Design by: Niko Magaro
Editor: Kim Thompson
Series Development: James Earley

Photos: All images from Shutterstock

Library of Congress PCN Data
Ferryboats / Ryan Earley
How I Get Around
ISBN 979-8-8945-9262-6 (hard cover)
ISBN 979-8-8945-9276-3 (paperback)
ISBN 979-8-8945-9304-3 (EPUB)
ISBN 979-8-8945-9290-9 (eBook)
ISBN 979-8-8945-9318-0 (audio)
ISBN 979-8-8945-9332-6 (Read-Along)
Library of Congress Control Number: 2024946365

Printed in Canada/012025/CP20250101

Seahorse Publishing Company
seahorsepub.com

Published in the United States
Seahorse Publishing
PO Box 771325
Coral Springs, FL 33077